D0831545

LINDOS

by Sonia di Neuhof

"APOLLO" EDITIONS

Cover picture : Ascent to the acropolis, leg. 6
The new town of Lindos, leg. 23
The text of the book is the work of the archaeologist Sonia di Neuhoff.
The photographs by the artist Photographer «Hannibal».
The publishers: E. Tzaferis A. E., Fokionos Negri 52, Athens.

LINDOS

The landscape of Lindos is one of the most beautiful in the world. A gigantic rock (height 116 m.) rises abruptly from the sea creating an unforgettable impression on the visitor. Everything up there is flooded with a dazzling sunlight against the blue background of sky and sea. The view is indeed breath - taking. Two harbours, a larger and a smaller one, are formed to the North and South of the cliff. The acropolis of ancient Lindos occupied this rock, where the prehistoric female deity of fertility was worshipped since the very remote past. The cult continued on the acropolis in historical times and the sanctuary of Athena Lindia, famous in antiquity not only among the Greek but also the outside world, began to take form gradually.

History

Lindos is not a Greek name, nor were the first inhabitants Greeks. Their place of origin was Asia Minor and they apparently came on the island from the coast across. In any event, it is believed that, traces of human occupation dating to the Neolithic period (7000 - 2600 B.C.), are denoted by a limited number of movable finds brought to light by chance.

Greeks appeared for the first time in Lindos, as they did on the rest of the island, around 1500 B.C. (in the Mycenaean period), when the Achaeans were dominating the Aegean with their fleet and trade and establishing numerous trade - ports on Greek lands as well as on the coasts of West Asia.

The great era of Lindos begins from the 11th century B.C., in the early historical times, when the Dorians under the leadership of Tlepolemos arrived on the island, bringing along with them the cult of Athena. Then Lindos became the most prominent of the three centres of the island (the other two were Ialysos and Kamiros).

3

When the Dorian hexapolis was founded in the early 7th century B.C., the three great cities of Rhodes had already gained such imporrance that they became thee of its six members. The religious centre of the Dorian hexapolis was the sanctuary of Apollo on the Triopian cape of the peninsula of Cnidus.

Shortly afterwards — in 690 B.C. — the Lindians, who were able seafarers and traders, founded two colonies: Gela on Sicily, whose founder was the Lindian Antiphemos; the Cretan Entimos was the founder of the second colony was established on thecoast of Pamphylia, where the great and prosperous city of Phaselis was built. Phaselis was forced by Kimon to join the First Athenian Confederacy in 468/7 B.C., when he set off to attack the Persians on Eurymedon.

Lindos developed into a great naval power, thanks to the favourable geographic position of the island of Rhodes which lay at the crossroads of sea routes from East to West and from Asia Minor and the Greek islands to Egypt and Cyrene. The city maintained also important mercantile contacts with Egypt, Phoenicia and Cyprus, as attested by archaeological finds.

The naval development of Lindos and of the other two great cities of Rhodes was inevitably accompanied by progress in commerce which brought abundant wealth to the inhabitants of the city. It is precisely this position of Lindos that was the cause of its good, as well as often adverse, fortune in all periods. Whenever it became possible for the city to avoid invasions and develop autonomously, its dwellers, who were capable, progressive, hard - working and peaceful people, had all the prerequisites for a comfortable and good life.

The great glory of Lindos was Kleobulos, son of Euagoras, a

celebrated figure who ruled the city for 40 years in the 6th century B.C. He was the descendent of a great royal familu, a contemporary of Solon, and was regarded as one of the Seven Sages for his exceptional intellectual gifts. His was the famous saying «,μέτρον ἄριστον» («nothing in excess»). Kleobulos was famed as a politician. He waged wars against the dwellers of Lycia on the opposite coasts, and took great pains to give a monumental form to the very old, sanctuary of his city. According to the ancient tradition, in order to collect the money required for the construction of the temple of Athena Lindia, he composed the famous «χελιδόνισμα» (swallow song) sung by the children who went from house to house collecting money. (It is believed today that the song was a popular creation and that children sang it at the beginning of spring to welcome the arrival of swallows).

In 491/0 B.C., when the Persians stopped at Rhodes on their way to conquer Greece, the inhabitants of the island were compelled to seek refuge in the fortified acropolis of Lindos. The city was besieged by the enemy for a long time and faced the danger of surrendering because of lack of water, but was saved at the last moment thanks to the help of Athena Lindia, patroness of the city. According to the local tradition, the goddess saved the besieged people by sending a grey cloud which stood above the acropolis and disolved into rain. Witnessing this divine intervention ,the barbarians were frightened; they dedicated rich offerings to the sanctuary of the goddess, became friends with the Lindians and sailed away.

In the naval battle of Salamis, the Lindians together with the other Rhodians were forced fo fight on the side of the Persians. However, when the defeated barbarians left Greece, Rhodes made haste to join the First Athenian Confederacy wishing to secure itself against the Persian menace.

In 408 B.C., the three great cities of Rhodes were united («synoe-cism'») and most of their dwellers settled in the newly founded city of Rhodos. Henceforth, while the other two cities fell gradually into oblivion, Lindos continued to be prominent owing to its ancient sanctuary of Athena Lindia, which was a great religious centre of Rhodes, famous all over the ancient world; aven the Pharaohs of Egypt honoured it with rich offerings (Amasis in the 6th century B. C.).

From the age of the synoecism the history of Lindos follows the general pattern of the history of the island. Some Lindian scho-lars are known from various periods, such as Timachidas, son of Agesitimos, historian and philologist. He is worth of special atten-tion as he is the writer of the «Chronikon» (Chronicle) of the shri-ne of Lindos which was engraved on a large plaque (in 99 B.C.). It records the most celebrated dedications offered to the sanctuary and the most important miracles of Athena Lindia. This inscrip-tion was found in the course of excavations and is now in Kopen-hagen (it measures 2.37 X 0.85 m.).

On his return to Jerusalem, during his third apostolic mission, Paul the Apostle, landed on Lindos - where the winds had carried the ship on which he was sailing from Ephesos - on the 25th April of A.D. 58. The little bay where he landed is today called «St. Paul's harbour» and there is a small post - Byzantine church dedicated to his memory.

In the 10th century A.D., another Lindian scholar, Constanti-nos, known as Constantine the Rhodian, studied in Constantino-ple and became a «grammarian»; later, in about A.D. 920, he ente-red the court of emperor Constantine Porphyrogenitus as a royal priest. A devoted Christian, he was opposed to the ancient religion and scoffed at his compatriots for the worship of Athena. In his work has been preserved an important epigram of the 3rd or 4th century A.D., referring to the olive trees planted in the sacred grove of Athena by ther priest Aglocharos. This epigram, known only from ancient sources, was found carved on the west side of the, rock of the sanctuary. (The Hellenistic age was a period of great flourishing of the shrine).

There is no data regarding the mediaeval history of Lindos; only the names of some scholars are known. The acropolis was used by all the foreigners who set foot on it and occupied it: the Knights of St. John, the Franks and the Turks. Hence, they maintained and occasionally repaired its fortifications. In 1592, Sultan Suleiman the Magnificent became master of the island of Rhodes. Following the Turkish domination, Lindos apparenrly continued leading an active life with its commerce and navy. Considerable wealth must have collected in the city, to judge by the beautiful houses that have survived, dating to the 16th and 17th centuries. These are noteworthy architectural constructions of hewn blocks of fine local stone, built by native artisans in a remarkable combination of elements from the architecture of the period of the Knights and the popular style. Especially characteristic are the façades of the lordly houses - dwellings of Lindian shipowners in the period of the Turkish domination - with elaborate relief ornaments on the walls and windows, and attractive decorative patterns on the mosaic floors (mawinde of seapebbles) of the courts as well as the interior of the houses.

Visiting Lindos

Today, the first and main purpose of a tour of Lindos is the, visit of its impressive acropolis, where the ruins of the sanctuary of Athena Lindia are located.

After passing through the lower gate of the mediaeval wall, the visitor reaches a terrace (No. 1), where hewn out of the rock is a circular exedra and a relief ship (A). The inscription on the latter indicates that it was the base of the bronze statue of Hagesandros. Dating to 180 B.C., it is a work of the Rhodian artist Pythocritos, who also made the relief of the ship (the stern is depicted). The reason for the foundation of this work is unknown (perhaps some, unknown naval victory of the Rhodians).

The inscription of the priest Aglochartos is carved on the rock on the left side of the exedra.

Leaving this terrace and climbing the stairway of later date, the visitor reaches the second terrace of the Acropolis. On the right are the ruins of the Commander's Palace (No. 3) of the mediaeval fortress. By its South wall is the ruined three - aisled church of St. John (No. 4). A multitude of offerings stood on this terrace - especially in the Hellenistic period which was an era of great prosperity for the entire island of Rhodes. We learn about the votive offerings from the Chronicle of Timachidas and the numerous inscribed bases found on the site.

In the Hellenistic period, when the sanctuary of Athena Lindia took its final form, a great Doric stoa (No. 5) was constructed, (around 200 B.C.) on the North side of the sanctuary, along nearly the entire width of this terrace. Some of the columns have been restored. The central section of the Stoa included the stairway, built earlier at the time of Kleobulos, leading to the temple which stood on the higher terrace. Later, the old stairway of the archaic period was covered by the one we see today. It gave access to the great Propylaea .(No. 6).

The Stoa (No. 5) is Π - shaped; while its central horizontal part has a large width, its two vertical parts have a very small length (dimensions; 88 m. length, 8.90 m. depth, with 42 columns on the façade. The edifice had a height of 6.20 m.).

After the synoecism of 408 B.C., were constructed great Propylaea (No. 6) serving as a monumental entrance according to the rule of that age. The great Stoa and the Propylaea completely separated the sanctuary of the goddess from the rest of the acropolis. The Propylaea of Lindos remind in general lines the Propylaea of the Acropolis of Athens. Their cross wall has passages, while there are rooms in every direction - front, rear, right and left. From the two side - wings, which are vertical to the cross wall of the Propylaea, the Western one has a greater number of rooms and its South end extends as far as the wall of the acropolis.

After crossing the Propylaea, the visitor stands in front of the temple of the goddess (No. 7). This edifice was built after 342 B.C., when the archaic temple founded by Kleobulos had been destroyed by fire. The same fire burned the old wooden cult statue of the goddess.

The very ancient local legend of Lindos records that when Danaus and his daughters fled from Egypt, passing from the island of Rhodes on their way to the Argolid, they founded the shrine of the goddess and her wooden statue around 1510 B.C. Pindar's information regarding the history of the island (in his 7th Olympian Ode) corroborates the local Rhodian legend according to which the cult of the goddess on the site of Lindos is earlier than the settlement of the Dorians on the island. From the foregoing it becomes apparent that originally the great prehistoric female deity, probably named Lindia, was worshipped here. Later the Greeks named her Athena Lindia (the Dorian inhabitants who brought along with them the cult of Athena). The goddess was initially worshipped in the grove of the acropolis, which was tended by her priests in all ages until the ancient cult was extinguished. The first statue of the goddess, the one dedicated by Danaus, was a «xoanon» of unworked wood. There was no altar, nor were blood sacrifices performed on the acropolis, as they were elsewhere. The dedications of the faithful were «fireless offerings» fruits, cakes, drinks.

In the late Geometric period, perhaps, a small Sekos was built for the goddess and a small wooden statue was dedicated to her.

It represented a seated figure crowned with a wreath and wearing a garment with ornaments («hormoi»).

As was customary in his age, Kleobulos renovated the shrine of Athena Lindia. On the highest part of the rock was erected a, larger temple, probably similar in plan with the one that survives at present. It was a Doric temple with four columns on the façade and four in the opisthodomus. This edifice is probably overlain by the later temple erected when the archaic building was burned in 342 B.C. The sanctuary then acquired a new acrolithic statue of the goddess; the body was of gilded wood and the head extremities of marble or ivory. The goddess was represented standing. In her right hand she was holding a «phiale» (bowl) and in her left, hand she was carrying her shield. A wreath crowned her head and a necklace adorned her breast.

The temple we see in our days has its walls preserved - some of its Doric columns have been restored. It measures 22.40 X 7.80 m. The sekos is closed in the opisthodomus. At the North corner of the temple, in about A.D. 200, one of the Seleucids founded a small shrine to the oracular Psithyros god Psithyros.

Excavations were undertaken in Lindos by Danish archaeologists and the most important movable finds are now in Kopenhagen, while others are exhibited in the Museum of Constantinople.

During the Italian occupation of the island restorative work was carried out in the momuments of the acropolis.

Monuments outside the acropolis

Present - day Lindos offers a most pictoresque sight as it spreads at the foot of the acropolis. Worth seeing is the church of Panaghia of Lindos, constructed in the 15th century by d' Aubusson; it is a crufiform building with octagonal dome. In the porch before the West side entrance is the bell - tower with the coat of arms of the Order of the Knights and d' Aubusson. The walls of the church are covered in the interior with paintings of the Symian artist Gregoris (in 1779, according to an inscription above the North entrance). Outside this entrance there are wall - paintings dating to 1675.

The greatest surpise in the present town of Lindos is the visit of its old houses, where one can admire many antique Rhodian plates and wooven fabrics.

On the West slope of the acropolis is located the ancient theatre of Lindos. Only the cavea and orchestra have been preserved. Nearby, next to the church of St. Stephanos. there are traces of, the ancient Cymnasium of the city.

At the site Vighli, on the North slope of the acropolis, there is a small ancient shrine within a natural niche of the rock. It is the «Boukopion» (slaughter - place of oxen) and its name denotes its function. As already stated above, following the local prehistoric tradition, the Dorians did not offer, as it was their own custom before coming to Rhodes, blood sacrifices to the goddess on the acropolis. However, feeling the need to sacrifice oxen to the goddess, they did so outside the acropolis, in the Noukopion. Many of the inscriptions carved on the rock around the shrine refer to these sacrifices called «Boukopia» and performed in honour of Athena.

Finally, a large circular monument of the Classical period consisting of blocks of ashlar masonry standing of a slightly wider base, is known today as the «Tomb of Kleobulos». It is located on the edge of the promontory to the North of the great harbour. Inside the building, a passage leads to a small rectangular burial chamber where the tomb is carved in the rock. Originally the monument was surrounded by a peribolos. The Christians converted it into the church of St. Aemilianos.

Note : The numbers in the text refer to the Plan on page 14.

LIST OF ILLUSTRATIONS

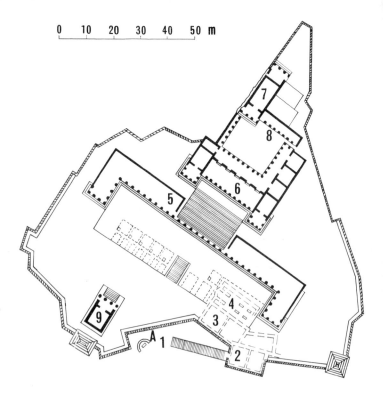

1. — Terrace from which the ascent to the acropolis begins.
1a. — Relief of the ship.
2. — Gate.
3. — Ruins of the Commander's Palace.
4. — Church of St. John.
5. — Doric Stoa of the Hellenistic period (200 B.C.).
6. — Great Propylaea.
7. — Temple of Athena Lindia.
8. — Closed peristyle court.
9. — Roman temple.

The following guides have been published by the APOLLON Publishers and can be obtained at the corresponding archaeological sites:

By the Archaeologists

Athens Byzantine Museum
Manolis Chatzidakis

Minoan Civilisation and Knossos Palace
Sonia di Neuhoff

The Acropolis and its Museum
M. Brouscaris

The Acropolis
M. Brouscaris

Copper Items of the Athens National Archaeological Museum
Basil G. Callipolitis
Efie Touloupa

Delphi
Sonia di Neuhoff

Ancient Olympia
Dora Karageorga

Ancient Corinth
Sonia di Neuhoff

Marble Masterpieces of the Athens Archaeological Museum
Dimitrios Papastamou

Vases of the Athens National Archaeological Museum
Barbara Philippaki

Mycenaean Collection of the Athens National Archaeological Museum
John Sakkelarakis

Cycladic Collection of the Athens National Archaeological Museum
Efie Sapouna-Sakkelaraki

Lindos
Sonia di Neuhoff

Mycenae-Mycenaean Art

Corfou

Epidaurus

ILLUSTRATIONS

MAP OF GREECE

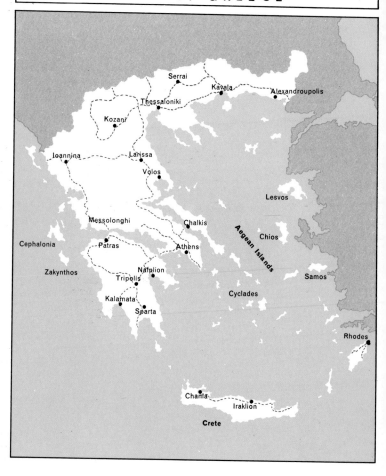

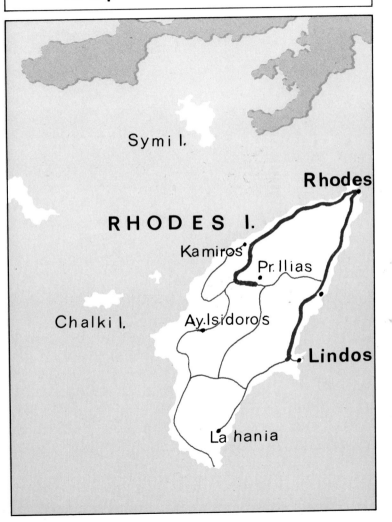

Map of Rhodes

Symi I.

Rhodes

RHODES I.

Kamiros

Pr. Ilias

Chalki I.

Ay. Isidoros

Lindos

La hania

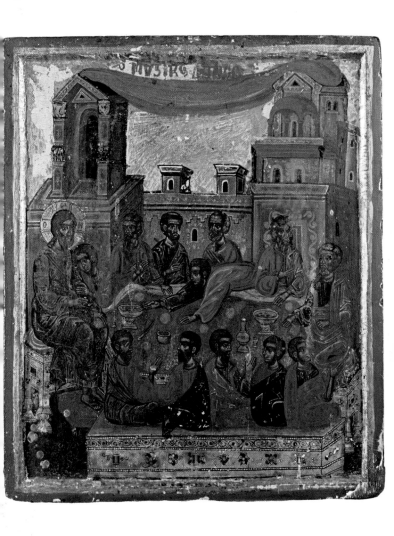